Do not believe that I am incapable

of bearing immense pain.

I have had a lifetime of it, and a

burden such as that can only be

wielded as a fierce weapon.

{Lifetimes}

I pledged I'd build a staircase
to the moon.
I planned, I dreamt.
I built and loved
those little steps.
The steps that lead me upward,
away to my moon.
I planned to use my staircase daily
to meet that brand-new view.
That night, they came in droves.
I thought to view my dream.
The axes and flames arrived, and
devoured the little steps.
For years, I sat in disbelief
mourning the pile of ash.
I sat firmly on the ground
admiring my moon afar.
One night, she said quite calmly,
"I understand your pain
and you think you're always stuck.
But my dear, you must understand
that dream you've wanted most
has always lived inside you.
You just must let it out."

{Staircase}

Into the depths
I go.
To find myself
and
save my soul.

{Depths}

Never will I pose.

For it is never a true representation of life,

the soul, or emotion. The best captures of

time have been during the most mundane

wanderings.

{Captures of Time}

Life is stolen from those who deserve it

the most. And while the rest of us wait in

the darkness, praying for the lights to

kiss us, the passed look down and

unburden us from above, whispering that

it will all be okay in the end.

{Stolen}

I used to hate those scribbles
my scratches on the page.

Failure, imperfection
are all they seemed to say.

They mock me as I learn
to truly become my own.

Those tiny little marks
could be my world alone.

Yet, I refuse my scratches,
those scribbles on the page.

They will not define the life I want,
the limits they impart.

No, the marks upon this page of mine
mean more than I can bear.

They show my pride, determination
to try and try again.

So thank you, little marks,
my scribbles on the page,
you showed my failure wasn't true
my determination stronger still.

{Scribbles}

I knew you were in there

under all the trauma

that buried you so deep.

Behind all the walls

that sheltered you from life.

I promise you that

little girl is finally free and safe.

Though older now, your life

is just now blossoming

with all the joy and possibility

that should have always been yours.

{Buried}

young and bright

light and life

trauma and pain

love and lessons

growth and failure

age and frailty

light and freedom above

mourning below

In the path of life
no one ever spoke of the pain of heaven.

{Pain of Heaven}

The past binds my soul in shackles,
fear and dread a gilded cage.

So safe a life they've made,
hope and life buried in the ruble.

Hidden deep so there's no air,
vulnerability comes in the night.

Small cracks in the facade
break and shatter the silence.

You find that hope has grown
in the futility and desperation.

Deep roots know their strength
and rise to hold the pain.

Step from that doorless cage,
it held no power over you.

...that lovely gilded cage

{Caged}

There is nothing more beautifully

transformative than watching the storm come

with all her strength and might.

And as you stand in the midst of her,

remember how invigorating it felt to have

survived her.

{Transform}

Thank you, little brain

for keeping me so safe.

You overthink, you pace,

you worry and analyze, all the problems that could ever be

just to keep me safe.

But my body is tired and weak

from all the "protecting" that you do.

I want to laugh and enjoy my life

the way I see others do.

So thank you, little brain, for everything you've done.

But I'm not in survival mode,

my time for joy has come.

{Little Brain}

There are magnificent worlds in your soul.
Don't ever give them up. Though the pressure
will come, bring them to the surface and bask
in the possibilities.
Don't ever become complacent.
Breathe joy; breathe the fire of Creation.

{Worlds}

Some days I wish I was like
everyone else.
To follow the designated path
that leads to guaranteed success.
Too damn bad
normality just isn't in my veins.

{Normality}

We always elate at the sun and how grand her
rise and fall are.
But, have we ever stopped to wonder about the
moon's glorious space in the night sky?
How little adoration is given to her
magnificent role.

{Night Sky}

Embrace your dark seasons. You have no idea
what they are trying to teach you.

{Darkness}

Restless in the early dawn,

we wake with thoughts of growth.

At war with ourselves over lack

because deep inside, we broke.

There is no sleep here child,

for our thoughts wrestled it away.

Arise to meet the light,

for she starts a new day.

{There is No Sleep Here}

How can it be that
every snowflake has a
beautiful arrangement,
so unique in its
grand design?
Yet, here we remain
fighting for worthless
conformity.

{Conformity}

The sun is the most
magnificent when
she is breaking
free from the storm
...and so are you.

{Breaking Free}

Why do we run from rest?
As if it is some ill-begotten
thing that will destroy us
if we get too close.
While the whole time
it beckons us to restore
ourselves from what is
truly killing us.

{Run}

How grandiose is this world of ours, yet we
understand so little of it.

{Understand}

Maybe everything that happens
in our lives
is just research for
the next phase, project, or
beautiful place that we have
yet to see.

{Research}

Fear seeps into all of us.

At first, it is but a pinprick.

Yet, now she has her hold.

As time creeps on

fear has made a home

of her host.

Her claws so deep,

tear her out my love

and drown her.

She has no place here.

{Fear}

Some days I wish I was shallow.

The depths I carry in my soul

weighs heavy.

A badge of honor that

no one can see.

{Shallow}

The strongest relationships
are forged in the trenches.
When life keeps bearing down on you
at a sickening pace.
That is where unbreakable bonds
are formed.

{Bonds}

The darkness may come to consume you.

But, my darling,

you've always

been the light to lead the way.

{Lead}

We were never lost.

We've been here the whole time.

{Lost}

As we travel through life
there's a nagging voice pulling us
to things that aren't meant for us.
It starts as a whisper
then continues to a roar, screaming:

NOT GOOD ENOUGH, MAKE MORE MONEY
COMPARISON, NEVER GOING TO MAKE IT
THE DREAM IS DEAD, BE REALISTIC
UGLY, TOO BIG, TOO THIN
NOT RIGHT, FORCE IT, EVERYONE
JUDGING

She is the ego,
targeted for self-preservation,
the comfort zone.
For too long has she held control,
the well-built home of self-loathing and
judgment.
The only hope to cage her
is to give the soul her power.
She is your only hero.

{Death of an Ego}

I fell, tumbling downward
til I found myself at the bottom,
in the valley, between two mountains.
I don't want to be here
but here, my strength builds
to climb the mountain before me.

{Valley}

You buried that little spark of yours

didn't you?

Because it was too much for some.

The spark so bright

it outshined the sun.

Now you're someone you don't even want to be.

So dull and dim

you blend with the rest of the world.

That little spark still lives.

Reignite, the world needs it.

{Spark}

Who are you?

Under the life

that has distracted you.

Left to succumb to society's grip.

I know you're fighting

to find the real you.

The you that feels like the sun.

Keep searching my love,

she's there, I promise.

{Who are you?}

I'll never fit inside your lines.
I was born to run with light.
My compass isn't broken
it just doesn't fit your North.
I'll follow my own path,
outside your little lines.

{Lines}

My brain tells me one thing,
to set the worrying pace.
My heart says quite another,
reminding me of joy.
I must ignore the fight inside me,
for it has nothing to really give.
I am here to create and love.
And that's where my joy shall live.

{Joy}

Why do we apologize when we show emotion?
As if it were some incredible inconvenience to others
that we show our humanity.
To apologize for being deemed "imperfect".

{Sorry,Not Sorry}

You're so perfect.
You do it all.
Have everything under control.
No one needs to help you.
You got it.
Yet, behind closed doors
You're exhausted and burned out.
You can't fix all the problems.
You're silence is a cry for help.
For years, you've been scrambling
to keep it all together.
And you are done, perfect no more,
and now you can be free.

{Imperfect}

I've always had this sense inside
that no one else can see.
Some days, my ego hides it
behind sarcasm and pain.
It always seems to know the truth
and the path that I should take.
It feels so light and joyous.
I wish to make it complete
and bestow it as my gatekeeper.

{Sense}

Life gave me a rule book
that didn't fit my soul.
I tried to play its game
and follow all the rules.
It never made me happy,
only forced conformity.
I placed that little book
squarely on a pile
and burned it
into little smithereens.

{Rulebook}

First I thought I had it all,

everything was as it should be.

Then my whole world exploded,

everything ripped out.

I tried hard to gain footing

sadly, it never came.

I felt ashamed and defeated

because you abandoned me.

I thought we were together in this.

I know that's what we promised

but you just took advantage.

And though it hurt like hell,

my heart has healed, and I've found another.

They made me feel hope,

blossoming into the real me.

I'm so glad you and I are separate,

for it made space for me to live.

{Separate}

Confidence and imagination

forged together

ignite the life hidden deep within us.

{Confidence}

The lightning in me

rages away

announcing the thunder

in my blood

"let me out" it screams

birth the light

within you.

{Lightning}

I thought you held all the answers,
so I chased you through the night.
I begged and pleaded for healing,
but it was nowhere near in sight.
This life keeps reminding me
that you were always there.
But, I'm done chasing you
I think I'll rest instead.

{Chasing the Night}

I'm both hiding and seeking
from this life.
Constantly running,
just to wait.

{Hide and Seek}

I looked at the great trees

and watched their leaves brown and fall away.

I asked these giants how they deal with loss.

They spoke,

"We know that to gain new life,

we must first outgrow the old

which is no longer serving our greater purpose."

{Great Trees}

I watched a little girl

standing by a window.

She berated, belittled, and screamed.

I inquired about the hatred toward her own reflection

and as she turned

I realized

that little girl was me.

{Little Girl}

I rise as others sleep.
Awoken by these midnight thoughts
that just won't let me rest
til I break them on the page.
I hope these midnight thoughts
give others a little peace.

{Midnight Thoughts}

Some nights my sleeplessness grows,
digging away at my rest.
I try to fight it daily
but I have come to realize
that maybe insomnia
is just my genius hour.

{Insomnia}

I always thought I feared being alone
due to the absence of another.
But in reality, I only feared my thoughts
the true bully of my soul.

{Alone}

I found myself in future thought
tossed back and forth with outcomes.
The band cross my head
tight with anticipation.
I realize now
I'll never meet my future
if I don't let her go.

{Future}

We act as if addiction is reserved for those "others,"
while our own anxiety lies low,
lurking below the surface,
eating away at us,
getting us addicted to its physical and mental abuses.

{Addiction}

I grew my dreams and passions
each one loved fiercely.
But slowly, over time
they were ripped apart and shattered.
Every time I reached for a new one
it stabbed me with shame.

Yes, these passions spun me into circles
chasing every one til broken.
The shame almost tore me in two,
each failure a reminder.

I grew to resent these broken passions of mine
until I realized they lit a new path,
opening a door into the great unknown
throwing me blindfolded off a cliff.
And now my shattered dreams line the path.

{Broken Passions}

New chapters of our lives
require deep metamorphosis.
The old veils must be continuously torn away
to reveal our new state of being.
This tearing of veils may require temporary pain and challenges.
But, once the new life is formed
the beauty and joy will outweigh the discomfort of change.

{Veils}

I thought I knew my way,
the traveler down in my soul.

I used the moon and starlight
to navigate the deep.

I lost my way a time or two
the light drowned by the storm.

I now travel with my scars,
revealing my true path.

The journey is quite intense
but I needed it nonetheless.

{Traveler}

We all are born without it,
that damned little shame.
But it quickly demands a presence,
persevering to make a home.
It burrows deep with spurs.
As you try to dredge it out
the poison quickly spreads.
Burn it to the ground, my dear,
watch the phoenix rise
and say farewell to all the dark.

What a tiny, little shame

{A Shame}

I've spent my whole entire life
pinging from here to there.
Always rushing, never engaging
all the love life had to give.
Through all the rush and anxious pace,
a tiny voice did call.
There is no peace in this race
of anxious thoughts and moving.
They steal your happiness and life,
make you move so fast it hurts.
Stillness is the path you seek,
the one your soul craves.
Fly quickly to the quietness,
the peace it offers saves.

{Stillness}

Take the longest breath you can,
sit so long it hurts.

Drink your tea with intention.

Watch the horizon
til the stars kiss the sun.

Let the water caress your naked skin.

See the morning wake you.

Move so slow you hear your heart.

Allow joy to embrace you.

Know this pace will take you where fast never could.

{Slow}

Living requires great risk.

Dreams require risk.

The heights, the depths both require risk.

Which one are you willing to choose?

{Risk}

We wrongly romanticize resiliency.

It always comes with great pain or hardship.

Yet, it produces blossoms

after the storms have come to destroy us.

These blossoms are even more beautiful and intricate,

letting their scars peak through.

To give others hope,

to show them there are always blossoms after storms.

{Blossom}

Some of us were left alone
grasping for the simplest form of normalcy.

{You're on your own}

After a lifetime
being something
other than ourselves
we experience immense pain
at the birthing of something new.

{Growing Pains}

You lost yourself in childhood.

It's time to find the real you again.

{Childhood}

You lost your confidence,
your sense of self.

No inkling of the multitude of gifts you possess.
Your heart fills you with dreams from long ago.

The head whispers "You can't,
you're not good enough."

It sounds the alarm,
IMPOSTER! IMPOSTER!

How dare you want something greater.

{Imposter}

Everyone spoke of joy
and the feelings that it evoked.

I believed it to be a myth
not existing for myself.

I didn't know one could lack this,
having it buried deep, deep down.

{Hidden}

I've spent my life as different people
dancing round in masquerade.

Switching masks
to appease the masses.

Losing myself
a piece at a time.

I don't want to leave me behind
at the expense of others' comfort.

So I think I'll quit this masquerade
and dance with myself instead.

{Masquerade}

The promise of a better tomorrow
holding on through the silent dark.

Knowing that Hope's light
is always around the corner, waiting for you.

Reach out your hand.
She's waiting to save you,
to take you higher.

{Hope}

How grotesque perfection is,
demanding so much from us.

Always feeding on the need to do and be.
Eating away at us for not being enough.

Fed by society, family, and fears,
it exists to control us.

Your perfection is simply defined by your existence.

{Demanding}

My brave little fighter
you stood on unstable ground.

Always protecting me from attack,
the walls raised high to keep them out.

"Must protect!"
You kept me in this space.

I honor you for your job well done
but, your service is no longer needed.

I'm ready to run in the sun,
reclaiming my childhood.

I need to feel joy and happiness again.

You're too tired from years of wear,
lay down your sword and shield.

Flow into healing my little fighter,
you deserve it after all this time.

{Fighter}

The poison of your past crept slowly,
taking piece by piece from you.

Madly, we crave peace and healing
but remember, they are slowly working.

Constantly curing the pieces of poison
like small landmines in your being.

{Poison}

We were always told to follow suit,
never break the rules.

To sit timidly,
watching from afar.

Admiring others paving a new path.

Gather strength from the naysayers, blaze a new destiny,
you little rulebreaker you.

{Break the Rules}

There's another version of yourself
you must find her; let her engulf you.

Run free, my dear, and let everywhere you touch
......sprout wildflowers.

{Another Version}

When life puts you in the in-between
sometimes it's hard to see.

The transition is hard and rough at times.

The not-knowing, always-questioning,
confusion around every turn.

Though sometimes, the in between
is where the best things start to grow.

{The In Between}

Desperately seeking, never finding,
trapped just below the surface.

I could feel you there, waiting.
I wished to pull you free.

Knowing you wanted to teach me
how to be me.

One day, I finally found you
trapped below debris.

Well, hello, my long-lost love
it's nice to see you again.

{Found}

Do not shame your mistakes and missteps
for they do not define you.

They were destined to find you
to create the beautiful creature that stands before you.

{Mistakes}

Even if I'm scared
I'll continue to jump and soar from those heights.
The ones meant to stop me.

{Scared}

I was everything at once,
the perfect specimen.

Society demanded - successful, pretty, smart,
but now I've torn that old facade.

I am reborn
and my, is she breathtaking.

{Everything at once}

My days move better now,
I move at a lighter pace.

I listen to the birds sing in the morning,
feel the warmth of the morning sun on my face.

I breathe in the cleansing air.

Yet, sometimes my past taps me on the shoulder,
tempting me to turn.

I acknowledge her presence,
appreciate her being.

But I'm not going back,
I won't give up this new normal for anything.

{Move Better}

You believe me to be fragile
on the brink of collapse and shatter.

My life has seen hardship, trauma
and it has seen joy and light.

At times, teetering on the edge of these two worlds.

I don't exist in a state of fragility
there is only immense strength resonating here.

{Fragile}

Hit so hard that life disappears,
everything blurry, no sense of direction.

Find your steps, one at a time.

You may stumble and fall
but those blurry lines
lead you to the most beautiful heights.

Restoring perfect sight
to move you to your incredible future.

{Blurry}

You are so different.
Never sensing or belonging.

Always trying and failing
to fit into others' definitions of you.

My love, you have been brought to this earth
to impart your immense gifts, wisdom, and healing.

Don't you dare cover it up
trying to look like everyone else.

{Others}

After years of survival
your days are different now.

You move more cautiously,
expecting the worst.

The mornings begin with a different edge.
Anxiety and worry kiss you awake.

Always blocking all the joy and pleasure
that desperately seek you.

You may be safe now
but you don't know how to act.

Things are different now,
take every day slowly.

Believe in a better tomorrow.
Healing takes time.

{Different Now}

Failure prohibited.
Understand the world before you're ready.

Pressure built.
Anxiety grew.

We need the answer now.

Perfectionism grew
to avoid the shame.

Be right ALWAYS,
if not...FAILURE.

You don't deserve to exist,
why are you here?

And the worst of it all,
we failed at being children.

{Failure}

I'm unsure of what your life has held.
Each of us carries a weight.

Pain, life, fear and loss,
you've seen it all.

I don't know what you've felt
but you are beloved
if no one has told you.

You are fiercely loved,
every inch of your scarred heart.

Regardless of what life has dealt you
your scars are magnificent.

They let more love in
and allow you to give breathe.

Rest assured, my beloved
you are safe now.

{Beloved}

You've lived with your pain
for a long, long time.

Ingrained in your soul,
it has taken residence.

Please unburden it,
let it fall away.

Your best life is waiting
and it doesn't need your pain.

I know you feel naked without it,
that pain was built into you.

You can't get that time back
but please hear me out...

The void that pain has left
can now be filled with life.

{Pain}

Healing is a wild thing,
your life runs on a different timeline.

Some days go up
and some go down.

You'll be happy with a glass of wine
and friends...

And next, be wrapped up,
isolated in my house for days.

But most of the time, You're just waiting around
for your packages to get delivered.

Love,
Your neighbor in the robe and slippers

Just excuse me; I'm healing.

{Weird}

I've cracked open
and poured it on a page.

All the pain I've locked inside
is now finally free.

I pray it seeks others
and makes them whole.

Little did I understand
that I was built to move mountains.

So after all this time,
this pain serves a purpose.

{For You}

Gasping for air,
no light is here.

Disconnected to life,
everything tight.

I'm falling, falling
way, way down.

Can't stand
Can't walk

Depths binding me,
I can't find my path.

Who put me here?
I've been lost for years.

Is anyone coming to save me?
All I can see is that it's a long way down.

{Long Way Down}

I've looked around
wondering how I got here.

So far behind,
left in the back of the race.

Others on the horizon
enjoying life...living.

While I'm here, floundering,
unsure of how to thrive.

My soul filled with holes,
left loving them myself.

As the race continues,
maybe others got a headstart.

I had to stitch myself together,
and I realized that was my strength.

Those scars showed me worlds I never knew,
paving new roads for those behind me.

So, in the end, there was no competition.

{Competition}

To those we lost to Covid,
we never got to say goodbye.

We never saw it coming
and the toll it took on us.

Shattered us into a million shards.

Never allowed to grieve or touch.
It stripped us of our cultural identity,
and of our humanity.

{Nineteen}

Others stigmatize,
believing that it defines us.

It can be all-consuming
and also interfere at the oddest times.

It could hit during joyous occasions
or overtake at sleep.

Life seems to float by,
condemning us to the sidelines.

{Depression}

There is a fire deep within you,
it shifts and rages away.

Channel that extraordinary energy,
use it to change the world.

{Energy}

Two lovers' dialogue

under a midnight sky, huddled round a fire's warmth.

"But who takes the time to look up at the stars?"

Sighs

"Only us dreamers."

{Conversations of Dreamers}

She was born to be the finder of ways,
constantly searching, pruning others for the life they seek.

Her seas were rocky,
she envied others.

Yet, over time she realized...

She was here to provide shelter,
to guide others onward.

{Way Finder}

When deep in pain and hardship
remember this rule.

Difficulties have a deadline.

And when you start questioning your potential and dreams
remember this...

Not a single thing in this world is ever impossible.

{Life Reminder}

A loved one once observed me
living day in and day out.

Always feeling kind of numb,
just the daily routine.

One day they said:
"You're so in your head you can't enjoy anything; as soon as you leave
it, you'll be free."

And ever since then, I've left my overthinking alone.

{In Your Head}

I've been living in gray,
seeing only the survival of it all.

Now that I am thriving,
I see the vivid colors.

My eyes are finally wide open.
Adoring and absorbing all I see.

With childlike wonder
I see all of the beauty I've missed.

{Eyes Wide Open}

Blooms, but appear for a short time every year
and for the rest, sit dormant.

With no beauty adorning the branches.

But in perfect time, she releases her beauty,
the magnificent splendor that is worth all of the waiting.

{Bloom}

You may have chains that weigh you down,
threatening to take you deep below.

Keep pushing onward.
Life's too short.

Besides, you have too many fabulous things to accomplish.

{Chains}

Life comes in all different shapes and sizes,
the paths are never straight.

Everything shifts and alters
with every twist and turn.

My size and strength reshape with all that life throws at me.

{Different Sizes}

I watched incense burning,
the wisps of smoke being tossed here and there.

I must take a lesson from these ethereal wisps,
for they know the meaning of life.

To allow the winds to gently carry you
to your next destination, simply allowing, never forcing.

{Wisp}

I tried to fill the deep void with materials,
the items that ultimately owned my love.

Then, they faded, and I lusted again to fill the void.
The unending cycle of want and emptiness.

What will save me from this viscious cycle?

{Void}

A decade, or even a few years ago, I would've begged you to tear away this pain.

But now, in this present moment, in my healing state,
I will forever be grateful for the lessons that it bestowed.

{Grateful}

The menagerie in perfect step,
listening to the sound of the whip.

Go here, stay there,
perform the perfect trick.

On display for the world to see,
the ringmaster barking orders.

{Circus}

Thank you for being.

Not for any particular shape or size
or beauty of skin.

Not for intelligence, job, title, or money.

Thank you for your existence.

For bringing your beautiful self into the light
so the world can admire your strengths.

{Thank you}

In the dawn, in the first light, where we witness
the sun kiss the sky.

My, what a scene to behold.

{In the Dawn}

Loss is a harsh teacher.

At times, God picks the most beautiful of his wildflowers
and we must learn to say goodbye.

Knowing that wondrous blossom is now in heaven's garden.

{Loss}

Let the sun etch the biggest dreams onto your soul
then go forth and shine on others.

{Etching}

I made my feet find rhythms I didn't know existed,
that were unbeknownst to me.

{Dancing}

Assuming that my life should look like yours?
How brave of you.

I have no want nor reason for my life to be like yours.
To take away my creativity and plan for life

This grandiose vision of ideas,
that tap dance in my head at night.

How dare you laugh at my plans
to make my life extraordinary.

.....the plans that are currently still forming,
but are there nonetheless.

{How Dare You}

I placed a very specific order for life,

back when I was just a child.

Making such demands and dreams seemed easy.

I watched others do it all the time,

...while I'm still waiting on the mail.

{On Backorder}

Life taught me how to row at an early age.

The only problem...

I wasn't prepared for the Colorado

on a pool float.

{Row}

Years of not fitting in anywhere
made me feel unsuitable.

The wrong puzzle piece in the box.

Come to find out
this world wasn't built for me.

I am meant to create my own
...with crayons and construction paper if need be.

{Not made for me}

Through every stroke of pain and helplessness,
every hard day and tear-filled night,
the months the emotions wouldn't slow down,
the years that didn't provide sleep.
With every stroke life gave,
a masterpiece was born.

{Masterpiece}

Throughout time I've danced with versions of myself.

Some were ugly-triggered by everything.

Some were lovely, filled with happiness and joy.

Rushing through them to reach the "best" one, is my sole regret.

Not loving each and every one in their own beauty and time.

{Versions}

I've reached parts in my journey where I thought I was healed.

Til some jerk comes by and triggers my trigger.

Heres to the journey
and the "jerks" that are helping to heal you.

{Jerks}

I've always carried my baggage on my back
...til I found out it had wheels.

{Wheels}

I appreciate all the energy you give,
to make sure every little thing is okay.

But, in all that overthinking, don't forget yourself.

...and that glass of wine.

{To the over-thinkers}

My sight was restored to me,

as my life made its way through darkness.

Only then did I understand what true sight was...

To believe that something far greater than I lay on the other side of

the perpetual darkness.

{Restored Sight}

On a spring evening, I sat reading.

Amidst the lowering warmth of the sun,
I heard buzzing.

A small dollop of golden pollen befallen the page.

Thank you, little bee, for your most precious gift.

{Little Bees}

Swiping right, swiping left.

A smoother face, a thinner nose.

Fuller lips and brighter eyes.

Better hair, a smaller waist.

How dare this tiny screen
determine who I should be.

{Filters}

Somedays, I catch myself ungrateful and sour
over such meaningless inconveniences.

Then, I go outside
and my, how all of those inconveniences disappear on the wind.

{Gifts}

The human will is the strongest muscle in the spirit.

Never backing down, always going.

Seeking new life in what seemed like dead ends.

The Will is by far the core of existence.

Feed her correctly and she'll take you to mountaintops
you've never believed were real.

{Will}

The heavy sensation of silence
...what we've needed all along.

{Heavy Sensation}

Magic happens when you're brave enough to overcome what is anchoring you to fear.

There's splendor on the other side of
all the things holding you back.

{Magic}

Some days my reality doesn't match my dreams

and I catch myself wondering

...where's Amazon at, I need to return this.

{Reality}

Frustration seems to seep into
every facet of my life.
Frustrated at the lack of
consistency, the substitutions of
my grocery pick up, those that rely
on me, the way people honk
driving by, the face in the mirror,
the lack of progression, the broken
promises, the spilled tea, the way
the sun shines in my eyes, cleaning
the house...
Reflection upon this list invokes
guilt.
How dare I be so ungrateful.
But then I think, being frustrated
is human.
It's okay.
The accumulation of life's little
inconveniences can grow
wearisome.
For we exist in the fragility of our
own humanity.

{Frustration}

As painful as it was,

the past gave me the deepest insights into a reality I didn't know existed.

An existence that I would have been ignorant of otherwise.

{The Past}

There is nothing more awe-
inspiring than the rush of a bird's
wings.

It transports you to another world.

Take me with you, feathered one,
high above the chaos of this world.

{Above}

Allow all of your magnificence to
burst forth onto the world's
canvas...

The depths of your mind, the
empathy of your soul, the glorious
colors you keep locked away...

For if others deem you too much,
they can simply avert their eyes.

{Magnificence}

Every time I think I'm healed and
whole, life breaks and cracks me
open even further,
making me more alive than ever
before.

{Cracked Open}

Appreciating the light that filters
through my eyes,
allowing me to breathe in the wave
of colors and breathtaking sights.
To share a deeper connection with
other humans, with animals.
To focus on what I love to see and
process all of this beauty.
We are such complicated beings,
overcomplicating something that
was meant to give us unequivocal
joy and happiness.
Let us just simply see.

{Seeing}

Stop pushing yourself smaller just
because others are louder, bigger,
or deem themselves more
important.
Embrace everything that makes
you sparkle
then throw that glitter in the air.

{Confetti}

Yes, I am a beautiful being.
But beware...
I still bare thorns and fangs,
the innermost part of me has
touched flame.

{Beautiful Being}

There are multiple dimensions, the
depths within you my love.
Take every single one of them to
make yourself whole.
For life is but one grand experiment
waiting for the perfect culmination
of joy and passion to ignite your
inner spirit.

{Multiple Dimensions}

Live your life as if all of this shit
will be written in your memoirs
one day.
Make it interesting,
make sure you light that shit up
with failure, love, depth,
breadth..... actual living.
If done just so, your memoirs will
be a magnificent culmination of
grandiosity only known but to a
few.

{Memoirs}

The sun will rise again
even if you've been blinded by an
eternity of night.
It may take a week, a month, or
years
but I promise you it will rise again.

{Sun Rise}

I always admired the rebel in
others.
What they had the nerve to do, to
be, to accomplish.
Myself, not so much
just going through surviving, but
maybe all along that in and of itself
was the largest act of rebellion.

{Rebel}

Just remember, your beauty and
importance in the world never
diminished with all the hard and
ugly times you went through.

{Inner Beauty}

The scope of your existence is not
limited to the hardship that
threatened to deter you, the
trauma that disarmed your inner
being and sent you into survival
mode, the failed dreams, the
survival mode that is all
encompassing, the painful path of
healing.
None of these determine your
limitations in this breathtaking
world of ours.
Believe in your wild capabilities,
they have been instilled in you for
a beautiful purpose.

{Scope of Existence}

I'm so effing tired.
Brain won't function.
Fatigue day and night.
Hustle harder.
More caffeine.
Stay up late.
Be all the things.
Unfinished thoughts.
Stagnate dreams.

Welcome to burnout.

{Burnout}

I always asked for an extraordinary
life and she responded in kind...

"It won't be wrapped up in ribbons
and bows.
There will be stings and detours
along the way.
Periods of hurt and pain may
arrive without warning.
You will have to climb mountains
and cross rivers,
stripping you down to the barest
part of your soul.
Yet, great periods of joy will
abound from all directions.
Laughter so full, it will make your
head spin.
The deepest sense of joy flowing
throughout.
Love and peace filled days fill you
up.

...This, my love, is an
extraordinary life."

{The Extraordinary}

In this fast paced world of ours...
We have lost connection by gaining
isolation.
We have lost intimacy by gaining
technology.
We have lost vulnerability
by gaining egocentrism.

...We have lost our balance.

[Balance}

Get quiet...
Oh so quiet.
Can you feel it?
That small tickle?
Telling you to get up.
To try again.
To believe in your worthiness.
To gain that audacious dream
you've been chasing.

...Take heart, its coming.

{Tickle}

As I started to heal
I began unearthing my hidden
pieces.
Ones I had long ago forgotten.
Each and every one terrify me
as I meet them face to face.
A standoff that I must make.

{Terrified}

You've gotten good at hiding.
Keeping all your gifts locked
inside.
Scared to let them break you open.
To allow all the goodness you've
ever wanted to overtake you.
To shine so violently
that you glow in the dark.

{Hiding}

Let everything and everyone that
has ever held you back
be stones beneath your feet.
To send you skywards.
To the most amazing future.
The only future you ever deserved.

{Deserving}

There is nothing in this world
quite like you.
A beautiful soul, that has turned
barriers into fireworks.
All the love you're giving
is like the brightest prism of light.
The way you walk into a room.
Life itself emanates from every
step you take.
Look to the stars my love
and watch the heavens part.

...for there is no one quite like you.

{Like You|

We tend to look back with how
good it was.
But what if we looked to the future
that way?
Reach for the next beautiful thing,
the next best thought and feeling.
It will take you miles further.
Don't be stuck in the good of the
past.
For it doesn't just live there,
it is in your future too.

{Reach}

The impermanence of life marks
its precious nature.
That small dash between your
years, forge it into a circle.
So all those who come after
will see the impact of your life.
All the love and life you gave
comes into full circle,
lasting generations to come.
Should that not be the purpose of
life?
To empty yourself of everything
you are into the world.

{The Line}

To the intuitive, the feelers, the
deep thinkers.
Those who feel the energy, the
heartbeats of every living thing.
Please allow yourself to rest, to be
misunderstood,
to breathe slowly, intentionally.
Block out all the noise in the world
and become one with yourself once
more.

{The Feelers}

The human instinct of the unknown
only manifests itself as fear...the
uncertainty.
And the only way to combat this
overwhelming manifestation is to
embrace it, head on, without
trepidation.
For it is the enemy of your future.

{Instinct}

Remember, when in writing and
living life
the first draft may have some
bizarre shit in it.
But, it is also how the best stories
and art are created.
So please write your first draft.

{First Draft}

I've often wondered how wonderful
it would be if the lives of every
single person on this beautiful
earth were perfect for them.
And then I realized if that
occurred, no magnificent change
would happen, no achievements
would exist. So even if our lives
are less than what we'd imagined
maybe that's the catalyst for
change.
The tiny sparks attempting to
ignite a flame into something
greater.

{Perfection}

The best way of healing...

To play and have childlike joy.

For it reveals your inner child,

who has been waiting for so long

to come out and live again.

Breathing life back into you,

reminding you of what you really

are.

{Play}

Our entire life has been made up

of acts of rebellion to constantly

seek freedom.

Freedom of time.

Freedom from oppression.

Freedom of finances.

Freedom from societal

expectations.

Freedom to live.

In our actions to seek freedom,

let us not allow our lives to pass us

by.

{Freedom}

The brain has never yet in human
history
been inundated with constant
stimuli, til now.
We have been unguarded, naive in
allowing this assault on our well
being, our human existence.
We have become the
DISTRACTED.
Assuming we have lived a "full life"
based on the algorithm that has
dictated it so.
We can not indulge in human
bonding without the distraction by
our side, consistently reminding us
of what we could be, what we
should be.
Going here, being there, buying
this, cancelling that.
Allowing it to make a host of us.
The more we struggle, the deeper it
burrows.
Til one day the DISTRACTED
become the BLIND.

{Distracted}

The flash of inferiority.

The deep flare of anger.

The sharp stab of shame.

The writhing embarrassment.

The bristling intimidation.

The twang of bitterness.

My what a ravenous beast jealousy
is.

Beware my beloved, she feasts
incessantly.

{Jealousy}

The heavy among us are weighed
down by wisdom, truth, empathy,
love and immense pain.

We become ever laden with this
burden because our mouths have
been sewn shut.

To remain ever silent to all the
intricacies we feel.

Heavy lives inside us, entrenched
within our being.

She chooses but a few to endow
with this "gift".

We wait patiently to feel ourselves
become whole.

{Heavy}

Spirit born above the clouds.

Run free child.

Your ability far surpasses those

who wish to stay on the ground.

Run with the clouds.

Bask in the sun.

Embrace your spirit.

{Run Child}

Your spirit, life, and joy were too
much for this world.

The happiness you passed on...
beautifully embraced us all.

We arrogantly assumed you'd be
with us forever.

Taking time for granted,
as if we have eternity.

None of us believe we will heal
from this.

It took you so quickly.
Yet, you never wavered in
strength.

Now your soul smiles down on us.
Staying with us at every step.

We will be together again,
to chase forever.

{Gone}

You found your strength in
younger years.

Believing there was better,
right around the bend.

Never giving up, even in the face
of giants.

No. You stared them in the eye,
roaring til they collapsed.

Shattering,
cracking the ground in two.

The chasm birthing a new life,
one free from shame and guilt.

Keep onward,
roaring at your giants.

{Roar}

In the throws of survival
we caught a glimpse of sunlight.

Blissfully unaware,
in the center of it all.

And all at once it came down.
Hail. Wind. Rain. Lightning.

We stood in ignorance,
numb from the years.

Standing in danger,
we watched the storm.

Silently awaiting the sun.

And after all this time,
we kept pushing through it all.

{Tornado}

Some of us must rise
in the dark morning.

To race our demons to the awaited
prize.

Tricking the mind, before it has time
to start creating those demons.

Trying to give a chance to arm
ourselves
against our self-created beasts.

The morning sees the bright hope
arise,
giving way to strength.

{Morning Creature}

Don't look down.

Look up, look around you, look inside.

But, whatever you do don't look down.

For that is where you will find yourself.

{Don't Look}

Can we not honor ourselves
without stabbing others with guilt
and shame?

To temporarily blind them to our
own insecurities.

To vibrantly enhance their own
flaws,
so that our vulnerabilities stay
hidden.

{No honor}

Death is a pitiful thing.
She wreaks havoc amongst the
living.

Yet, offers peace to those who
passed.

She drags the living to the edge of
breath itself,
ravaging them in the throngs of
grief.

Yet, she gratefully embraces the
gone,
lovingly ushering them to a
beautiful new life.

While we deny and abhor her,
she is but another celebrated part
of life.

A new chapter for us all.

{Death}

We think that fragility marks us

for an ill-fated future.

But, perhaps it ensures that we live

full, unadulterated lives.

Where all of the fragile cracks are

fulfilled with beautiful memories.

Stories to pass down.

{Fragility}

No matter the accumulations we
seek, the possessions, the events,
the status, the power, the wealth.

It all is meaningless unless you are
generous with your talents in this
world.

Understand, that your presence is
meant for the betterment of
mankind.

{Compassion}

Life is but a blank page.

Though some have been crumpled,
never to return to their original
form.

Some burned, never to be whole
again.

Some discarded, for others hoped
they would become nothing.

And some who remain crisp and
clean without blemish.

Yet, it is the ones that have
withstood trials that often tell the
most magnificent stories.

For no one is interested in a
Crisp. Blank. Page.

{Blank Page}

Why is it that we so effortlessly
watch the human condition
continue to follow the same
destructive path as it always has?

Where are the brave souls ready
to stand alert and take charge of
altering the course of history?

To lay new pathways to a better
way of being human?

{Effortlessly Watching}

Trauma strips you of all the things
you thought you could be, you're
worth, all the things you never
had.

Strips you down to bone, making
you warp into an entirely different
creature.

You are worth all of the
magnificent things you watched
others receive.

You are worth every ounce of joy
that life has to offer.

{Stripped Away}

The road less traveled is just that,

a lonely path that often is rift with

hardships that at times you must

face alone.

Take heart though, for the ones

who have traversed this path

before are some of the most

beautiful souls.

And once you travel this path, it

will forever be ingrained deep in

your bones.

{Less Traveled}

Don't wake me up from my reality,
for it paves the way to my dreams.

Others flee from life's problems,
while I embrace them.

For it pushes me onwards to
greatness.

For as nice as thoughts are I would
never wish to live in them and call
it a life.

{I'll keep reality}

Walked outside to check on the

world, instantly regretting it.

She is so angry at every little

inconvenience, what am I to do?

Just little old me.

Embrace her with love, for it is

the only salve to heal such a deeply

inflicted wound.

{Checked on the world}

Those who mock simplicity will

never live in magnificence.

For if you can't love a simple life

how will you ever enjoy a great

one?

{Simplicity}

Reach out and grab the beautiful
things that make your heart sing.
Especially the ones sitting atop
mountains, which you are too
scared to grasp.
The ones you believe aren't meant
for you, the ones that bristle your
soul with electric...
Reach for them, they'll bring you
back to life.

{Beautiful Things}

The bravest of us need to be saved.

I know you're strong my love, but

allow yourself a reprieve from

your battles.

They are not all yours to fight.

{The Brave}

Trust fall.

Remember that game?

Well life's playing that with you

every day.

Are you willing to play?

Or will you continue to fight

against it?

{Trust fall}

We all have the ability to
experience everyday ecstasy.
Yet, we stay in a state of continual
exasperation.

{Everyday Ecstasy}

Becoming, in and of itself, is a

continual process.

We never stop becoming

something.

Our existence is linked to a

consistent push forward.

Unless, we have forcefully applied

the brakes, which only causes

stagnation.

{Becoming}

The maybes of this life are dream
stealers, life killers.
Never allow yourself to lay in the
maybes.
Move out of the somedays.
There is only today and you are
never promised a tomorrow.

{Maybes and Somedays}

The singular point of failure
for every tragedy, fight, and catastrophe
is that we are lost or simply uneducated in what love truly exists to
be.
Love is not an inanimate, stationary object.
A tangible thing we adorn on a shelf
or stow away so no one will ever find it.
Love is a verb, and it requires action.
It breathes, grows, or shrinks according to its environment.
And it will ultimately perish if not cared for throughout every stage
of life.
It will lose its splendor.
It will lose its zest for life.
It will give up on those whom it cherished most.
It only asks to be nurtured
through the simplest of tasks.
The brush of a lover's bare skin.
The kind words of a stranger.
The deepest understanding from a friend.
The compassion amongst the world.
Love doesn't require intensive labors
but, the consistent efforts of the human race.
And yet, we fail in numerous endeavors that require our love,
for it is too much of an inconvenience.
So we all tear away from each other in hopes of gaining a selfish
desire that we have substituted for love.
To the courageous ones who love,
you deserve the sky and all her wonders.
For you have bestowed a precious gift upon this world
and I pray that she returns it in kind.

{Love}

"You can't keep doing this." I
whisper to myself as I steal away to
eat another cookie...
Ah, the loss of willpower.

{You can't keep doing this}

I'll grasp failure by the face, kiss
her passionately and call her my
lover.

{Failure}

Why is it that we pervasively

fixate on the entirely materialistic

sphere?

Only stopping to try and breathe

after we've been crushed by the

weight of our things.

{Material}

Some days, I'd like to distance
myself from my life.
For at times, it feels like it will
swallow me up at any given
moment.
I keep spinning, only seeing the
abyss, waiting for the colors to
envelop me entirely.
Do others awake and love their
lives?
Or do they sit, as others do, behind
closed doors and bright screens,
attempting to convince the world of
their gilded lives.

{Distance}

Your brain triggers thoughts,

racing faster than the speed of

light.

You stop and yell.

"Stop that shit, its irritating!"

...Let's see if she listens this time.

{Faster than light}

Breathe life back into your being.

Let the day melt down your back.

Take an eternity to rest,

simply to heal.

Stop trying to convince yourself

that you must've accomplished an

extraordinary feat to earn rest.

{Convince Yourself}

We believe we don't have time for
life.
Our days move too fast.
Schedules too full with
unnecessary and unmemorable
events.
We miss all the things life is
begging to bless us with.
The flowers of spring, the coolness
of the ocean, the fluroescent colors
of the sun, the sparkling candor of
the moon and stars.
And though we fuss and strife over
such lack,
we are entrenching it into our
being.
The unfortunate disease of
absentmindedness,
no longer a side effect os sleep or
stress.
It is but a daily occurrence, a
lifestyle that is being embedded by
the choices we feel we can not
make.
Embrace a rebel's heart
choose to reject the idea of absence.
Embrace the wealth of presence.

{Absent}

Some of us know it better than
others.
The ability to put off what we
desire.
The strength to give it all.
The depth at which we love.
The sweat and tears we give.
The sacrifice we make.
All so our loved ones can live.

{Sacrifice}

There is a fleeting moment

when the earth is just rising,

while the rest of us slumber.

The elongated silence,

where everything is still.

Contemplating how to display her

beauty.

Go forward, meet her in this

moment.

For you will hear her heartbeat,

feel her breath on your skin

and have the most beautiful

conversations.

{Elongated}

I want to run, far away from here.

Til the sky and wind can't see me.

I get tired of fighting some days,

it burdens me with immense grief.

I mourn over my life and the

direction I wish it had gone.

Every time I rise from the ashes

another fire comes to consume me.

And though I am fierce,

I grow heavy, from years of wear,

burdened by life's flames.

So weighed down that if I touched

water I would drown.

So set me free and let me run,

far away from here, so that my

bones may rest.

{Far Away from here}

We act as if love is a trivial thing
to only be obtained by some
important few.
Placed on a pedestal for all to see.
Yet, no one speaks of what it really
is.
It is the hardest job you will ever
undertake.
The selfless time you give to
another.
It is the fights you have to show
you'll never give up.
The act of making another feel
pure, unadulterated joy.
To care so much more for the inner
being or another's soul.
It is collaborating, not
compromising, to gain life's
fulfillment.
The tearing down of trauma, pain,
and barriers, to build stability,
strength, hope and happiness.
It is the continual evolution of life
itself.
True love is not some mere trophy
to be won but, an action only taken
by a courageous few.

{Action Taken}

Perhaps, I am a little mad
but, what of it?
I have a hell of a lot more fun than
these "normal" people.

{Mad}

Excuse me, if I'm not in the same
place as many.
I was fighting invisible hurdles,
that were never in your path.
I tripped over many, but I still
made it.
Excuse me, if I take up more space
these days.
I am tired of hiding my light for
your convenience.
Though I feel "behind" the rest of
the world,
I now have much more to offer it
than you do.
So, no, I do not have many
"accomplishments" to my name
for I was building internal
strength.
Resilience that many of you simply
lack.
So excuse me, if I am not where
you're at in life.
Do not dare critique
for you were never in the arena
with me.

{Excuse}

Sometimes we must be plunged

into the darkness

to fully understand what the light

is.

{Plunged}

Watch life's punctuation.

Never place a period when a

comma would serve you greater.

Some of us need a semi colon

when we thought about stopping.

Learn your punctuation.

Despite what is written on the

page,

there will be times when you'll

want to forcefully put a period

but, I urge you to continue on.

{Punctuation}

I held my broken life up to the sun
and the prisms of light burst forth
into the most beautiful array of
colors.
The cracks and shards only proving
to create a more spectacular
masterpiece.

{Fragments}

For those of you where success did

not come easy or quick,

congratulations!

For you have learned to operate a

battleship while others a dingy.

{Success}

Remember when we ask for help or

guidance sometimes life sends a

storm to push us in the right

direction.

{Storms}

Most days I had a hard time

convincing myself that my cup was

either full or empty. Now, even if

all it bears is air, my cup is full.

{Full Life}

Triumph harder every day.
For yesterday is fraught with its
own complexities that can not be
undone.
Place high hope as a shield against
the thunderous condemnations of
this world.

{Triumph}

Edit your life ruthlessly,

for only there will you find

true authenticity.

{Edit}

www.ingramcontent.com/pod-product-compliance
Lightning Source LLC
Chambersburg PA
CBHW051421090426
42737CB00014B/2773